DATE DUE			
MAY 1 8 1995			

a visit to the BAKERY

℗ CHILDRENS PRESS ®

CHICAGO

by Sandra Ziegler

With sincere appreciation to the personnel at
COLONIAL BAKING COMPANY, North Aurora,
Illinois, for their cooperation in the photo-
graphing of this book.

And to the children who cooperated so
patiently as we recorded their visit to the
bakery on film.

Photography by PILOT PRODUCTIONS, INC.
  Dave Holmes, photographer
  Jay Kelly, lighting assistant
  Dean Garrison, director

Library of Congress Cataloging-in-Publication Data

Ziegler, Sandra
  A visit to the bakery.

  (Field trip books)
  Summary: A group of children visit a bakery and
observe how bread is baked.
  1. Bakers and bakeries—Juvenile literature.
[1. Bakers and bakeries] I. Title. II. Series: Field
trip series.
TX763.Z54   1987   664'.752   86-32647
ISBN 0-516-01495-1

1 2 3 4 5 6 7 8 9 10 11 12 R 95 94 93 92 91 90 89 88 87

a visit to the BAKERY

Created by The Child's World

"Hello, boys and girls. Welcome to the bakery. My name is Mr. Ross. I will be showing you how we make bread and buns."

Mrs. Belano's class smiles. The children want to see the bakery.

"You must each put on a hat," says Mr. Ross. "Everybody in the bakery must wear a hat."

Amy watches Brian before she fixes her hat.

First the children see where flour and other things used to make bread are stored. "Do you like white bread or brown bread better?" Mr. Ross asks.

"White," says Rachel.

"White bread, brown bread, and buns start out the same way," says Mr. Ross. "A baker puts flour, water, and yeast into a big mixer."

The children visit a mixer. "When the
flour, water, and yeast are mixed, the
mixture is called 'sponge.'" Mr. Ross says.
The children watch. The sponge will fall
out of the mixer into the black cart.

"See this other cart of sponge?" asks Mr. Ross. "Four hours ago, it didn't have much in it."

"How did it get so full?" Jeremy asks.

"There is yeast in sponge. Yeast makes the mixture rise.

"The baker is dumping a full cart of
sponge into this mixer," Mr. Ross tells
them. He points to the full cart, dumping
up above.

All the other things in bread—sugar, but-
ter, milk, salt—will go into the mixer too.
They will be mixed with the sponge to
make dough.

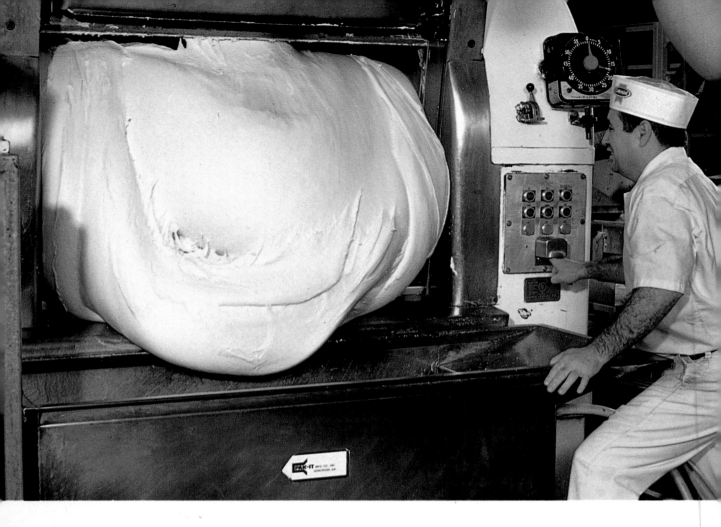

As the children watch, the mixer finishes mixing. The machine opens. It dumps the bread dough into another cart. The baker watches carefully. He makes sure the dough doesn't push the cart away and fall on the floor.

Another machine will grab big bunches of the dough. It will carry it up high where the children can't see it.

When the dough comes down again, it is
in little round balls. The balls drop into little pans.

"They are going away again," Andrew
says.

"Yes," Mr. Ross tells him. "But you will
get to see what happens to them."

"I think the machine squishes the dough," says Karen.

"Yes," says Mr. Ross. "First it flattens it. Then it cuts it just the right size for hamburger buns." Mrs. Belanos and the children watch the round circles drop from the machine.

The circles keep moving. They drop into
baking pans. Every row should have four
circles. Count them. Oops! Sometimes they
miss.

The bun pans move along to another
baker. He takes them off the machine and
puts them on a big rack. They are ready to
go into the rising room.

The rising room is so full of buns the children won't fit inside. So they go to see the
oven instead.

"The buns were in the rising room for forty minutes," Mr. Ross says. "The yeast and the heat made them rise again."

The buns are now ready to bake. The baker puts them into the oven.

15

"Look! Some buns are coming out of the oven," Amy says. "Mmmm! They smell good."

The children gather around to watch. "Now the buns look like buns," Beth says.

"The buns must cool now," Mr. Ross tells them. A machine lifts the hot buns off the pans. It puts them on a rack to cool.

The buns will cool as they ride along to the bagging machine.

Mr. Ross grabs some of the buns. He hands them to the children to eat. The warm buns smell good. They taste even better.

Next, the children see where the buns are sliced. "You can't see the knife," Mr. Ross tells them. "It is inside the machine so nobody will get cut."

He picks up a sliced bun and opens it.

As the sliced buns move along, baggers
are waiting. Each one grabs six buns and
slides them off the table. Six. Then six
more.

The buns never stop moving. They are on
their way to the bagging machine.

The bagging machine blows each bag open. The buns move right into the bag. Another machine puts a fastener on the bag.

"Neat," says Andrew.

"Yes," says Mr. Ross. "Now the buns are ready to go to the trucks."

The class visits the garage. "See all the trucks," Mrs. Belanos says.

During the night, bakery workers will fill each truck with bread and buns. In the morning, drivers will deliver them to stores and restaurants.

One driver has just come in with his truck. "Hello," the driver says. "Do you want to look in my truck?"

"Yes," the children say.

Sue and Maria climb into the truck.
Others just look inside. The driver shows
them how the trays slide into the truck.

Mr. Ross reaches into a nearby truck.
"These are for you," he says. He gives
Sue, Amy, and the others, tiny loaves of
bread to take home.

Then he finds some shiny pencils with the name of the bakery on them. He gives each child a pencil.

"You should be able to use these at school," he says.

It's time for the class to start back to the lobby. Mr. Ross stops for a moment in the bakery. "I have one more thing for you. I'll give it to you in the lobby," he says.

The children wonder what it can be.

"Don't you ever bake cakes?" Amy asks.

"No," Mr. Ross answers. "Other bakeries do that. We only bake bread and buns."

When the children reach the lobby, Mr. Ross gives them each a book.

"This is a book about making bread," he says. "It will help you tell your parents about your visit."

"Thank you," the children say. "It's fun to visit here."

Mr. Ross shakes hands with Karen's dad. And he tells the children good-by. He knows that the next time they eat hamburgers, they will think of their visit to the bakery.